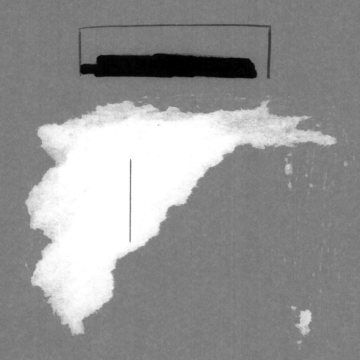

BRITAIN:THE FACTS
Law and Order

Christopher Riches

FRANKLIN WATTS
LONDON•SYDNEY

First published in 2008
by Franklin Watts

Design by bounford.com

Franklin Watts
338 Euston Road
London NW1 3BH

Franklin Watts Australia
Level 17/207 Kent Street
Sydney, NSW 2000

ISBN 978 0 7496 8380 1

Dewey classification: 320.441

Printed in China

Franklin Watts is a division of Hachette Children's Books,
an Hachette Livre UK company.
www.hachettelivre.co.uk

Picture credits
The publishers would like to thank the following
organisations for their kind permission to reproduce
illustrations in this book:

Cover image © Psl Images/fotolibra.

p. 6 © Metropolitan Police/PA/TopFoto; p. 7 courtesy of
Tandridge District Council; p. 8 bounford.com; p. 9 Julia
Quenzler/Getty Images; p. 10 © 2006 TopFoto;
p. 12 © 2002 Topham/PressNet/TopFoto ; p. 13 Ron Almog;
p. 14 © 2005 David Wimsett/UPPA/Photoshot/TopFoto;
p. 15 © 2004 UPPA/TopFoto; p. 18 (top) © 2002
Topham/PA/TopFoto, photographer: Fastfoto Picture Library;
p. 18 (bottom) © 2006 Guidance Limited; p. 20 © 2002
TopFoto; p. 22 UN photo; p. 23 postcards from British
Institute of Human Rights; p. 25 bounford.com.

All maps and diagrams © bounford.com.

Contents

The Law and Who Makes It

We have laws to say what is right and what is wrong. Laws also state what punishment should be given to those who break the law.

Our laws

Our laws consist of many Acts of Parliament and many rulings by judges on how these laws should be applied. The law is open to modification because it depends both on Acts of Parliament and on rulings in particular **cases** by judges who interpret the law.

How are our laws now made?

Laws are made by Parliament (see diagram). The words of the law have to be written very carefully so that their meaning is as precise as possible. There is a separate legal system in Scotland. The Scottish Parliament proposes and approves laws for the monarch to give assent to.

Hammurabi's code was written using an ancient form of writing called cuneiform, as in this clay fragment.

Early laws

Recording what is right and wrong has always been a concern of people. The Ten Commandments, revered in Judaism, Christianity and Islam, provide guidance, with such clear instructions as '*You shall not murder*' and '*You shall not steal*'. The earliest written law was the code of Hammurabi, the ruler of Babylon. It was written around 1780 BC.

When the Romans ruled Britain they enforced a clear legal code. After they left, this code was abandoned and laws were made and enforced by local communities. After the Norman conquest in 1066, royal courts became more powerful and out of their decisions came our system of law.

Creating laws

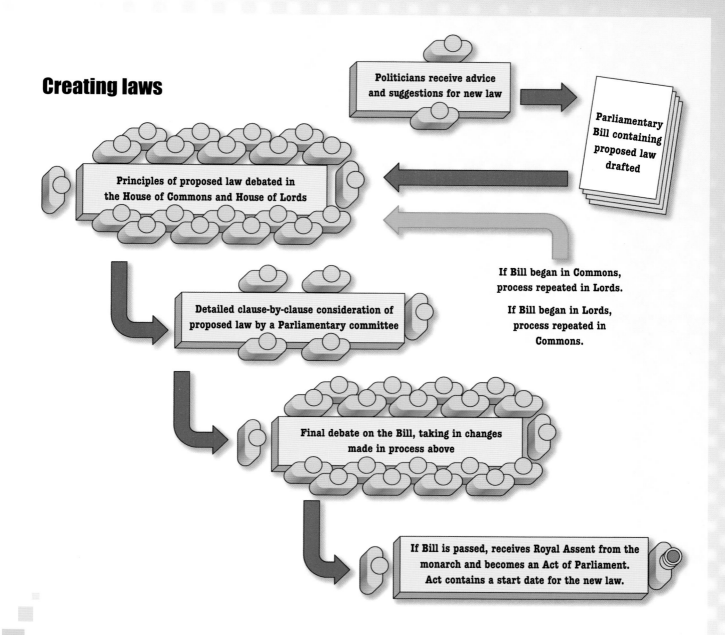

Politicians receive advice and suggestions for new law

Parliamentary Bill containing proposed law drafted

Principles of proposed law debated in the House of Commons and House of Lords

If Bill began in Commons, process repeated in Lords.

If Bill began in Lords, process repeated in Commons.

Detailed clause-by-clause consideration of proposed law by a Parliamentary committee

Final debate on the Bill, taking in changes made in process above

If Bill is passed, receives Royal Assent from the monarch and becomes an Act of Parliament. Act contains a start date for the new law.

Under our system of common law, our laws have been built up over centuries. There are many historic laws that, in theory, could still be enforced, for example:

⚖ In London, it is illegal to flag down a taxi if you have the plague.

⚖ In the city of York, it is legal to murder a Scotsman within the city walls, but only if he is carrying a bow and arrow.

⚖ In Chester, Welshmen are banned from entering the city before sunrise and from staying after sunset.

⚖ It is illegal to die in the Houses of Parliament or to wear armour there.

⚖ It is illegal to eat mince pies on Christmas Day.

Criminal Law

The purpose of criminal law is to provide rules to maintain social order and protect individuals and the community. People who break these laws are committing a crime against the State.

What does criminal law cover?

There is a very wide range of activities that come under the jurisdiction of criminal law. The main areas are:

 Violence against an individual (which can include murder, causing death by dangerous driving, wounding and endangering life).

 Burglary (breaking into a house and stealing things).

 Robbery (using violence to steal things directly from an individual).

 Theft (taking something belonging to someone else) and handling stolen goods.

 Fraud and forgery.

How is criminal law applied?

The police enforce the law.

▼

The police investigate crimes.

▼

When they have evidence, the police **arrest** those who they believe have broken the law.

▼

The police present this evidence to the Crown Prosecution Service (CPS).

▼

The CPS decide whether the case is taken to a court.

▼

The case is tried in court to decide whether the accused is **innocent** or **guilty**.

▼

The court has to assume that the accused is innocent. The prosecution has to prove his or her guilt.

▼

If found guilty, the judge sentences the accused. The **sentence** (punishment) can include prison, a **community order** or a fine.

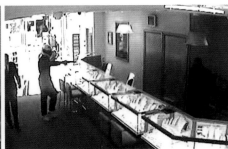

Images from a closed-circuit television recording. They show a crime taking place, and can be used as evidence in court.

- Criminal damage to property and arson (deliberately setting fire to something).
- Motoring **offences**.
- Child cruelty and child pornography.
- Sexual offences (including rape and prostitution).
- Using and supplying illegal drugs.
- Treason (spying and betraying the state).
- Terrorism.
- Being abusive or violent to someone because of their race or religion.
- Misuse of firearms and knives.
- Breaking trades description and public health regulations.
- Perverting the course of justice.

How old do you need to be to responsible for a crime?

- Up to the age of 10 (or 8 in Scotland), children cannot be held responsible for a crime.
- From the age of 10 to 17, children and young people can be arrested and **charged** with crimes as if they were adults. They will almost always appear in special youth courts.
- People aged 18 and over will be prosecuted in the normal adult courts.

Who investigates crimes?

The police (see page 10) investigate most criminal acts. In specialised areas Trading Standards officials, Environmental Health officials and Customs and Excise officers can prosecute. For example, if a shop is selling underweight goods, Trading Standards officials enforce the criminal law.

Making graffiti can be a criminal act as it damages someone's property.

Civil Law

Civil law covers many areas of daily life. A dispute in civil law is between two individuals or organisations. The State and the police are not involved. Punishments under civil law are financial.

How is civil law applied?

As civil law is used in disputes between two sides, the process of its application to solve a dispute is very different from criminal law.

1. The first step for the side starting a case is to take legal advice from a **solicitor** or a legal advice centre to see how the problem might be resolved.

2. Some disputes (for example, with a neighbour) may be better resolved with a **mediator** rather than in a court. There are a number of schemes to help people sort out disputes without going to court.

3. Disputes involving claims of £5,000 or less can be taken to the small claims court to get a judgment. This is cheaper and quicker than going to a full court hearing.

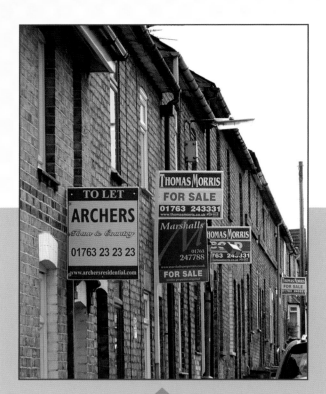

The procedures involved in buying or letting a house are laid down in civil law.

What areas are covered?

Civil law covers many areas where people are in dispute with each other:

Marriage, living together, separation and divorce.

Bringing up children (child care, education, medical treatment, **adoption**).

Death and inheritance.

Landlords and tenants.

Buying and selling a house.

Rights at work.

Supply of goods and services.

Disputes between neighbours.

The granting of **Anti-Social Behaviour Orders** (ASBOs).

4. If the case goes to a full court hearing, the **plaintiff** (the person bringing the case) has only to show that the defendant was more likely to have acted unlawfully than not. This is a less demanding test than in criminal law, where guilt has to be proved 'beyond reasonable doubt'.

5. The judge decides on who is telling the truth in a **judgment** (a formal decision) and can impose **damages** (a fine) that the guilty party has to pay the opposing party in the case. The judge can also make the guilty party pay all the legal costs of both sides of the case.

Because court cases can be expensive, many disputes are settled before a case reaches the court.

Solicitors and barristers

Solicitors are lawyers who deal with the general public and present cases in some courts, particularly in a Magistrates Court (see page 12). **Barristers** provide advice and appear in courts only when instructed by solicitors. Until recently only barristers could appear in a Crown and High Court (see page 12).

An artist's sketch shows the actor Michael Douglas watching his wife, Catherine Zeta-Jones, giving evidence at the High Court in London in 2003 in a civil case that involved the protection of their privacy.

The Police

The main role of the police is to prevent and detect crime.
The police also work to maintain public order.

The Bow Street Runners

The first organisation that we would recognise as a police force
was established in 1749. Henry Fielding was a **magistrate** in
London, based at
the Bow Street
courts (he was also
a famous writer).
As he could not
easily arrest
criminals to bring
them to court, he
started to employ
people to catch
criminals. They
became known as
the Bow Street
Runners.

Metropolitan police based
at Bow Street in 1888.

In 1829, the Metropolitan Police was
established in London by Robert Peel.
He required officers to wear a distinctive
uniform (to avoid confusion with spies,
it was alleged) and they were unarmed,
apart from a short baton. By the 1850s,
everywhere in Britain had a police service.

What do the police do?

The main activities of the police are:
- ⚖ Maintaining law and order.
- ⚖ Protecting people and property.
- ⚖ Protecting the country from terrorism.
- ⚖ Preventing crime.
- ⚖ Detecting criminals.
- ⚖ Controlling traffic on the road.
- ⚖ Helping in major and minor emergencies.
- ⚖ Assisting those who need help.

Police organisation

There is no national police service in Britain. Instead there are many local forces. Each force is managed by a police authority, most of whose members are elected councillors from the local government areas that any given police force covers.

Police officers

⚖ Provide a reassuring presence in the community.

⚖ Prepare evidence for the Crown Prosecution Service.

⚖ Are mostly full-time officers.

⚖ Are supported by volunteer special constables.

Police Community Support Officers (PCSOs)

⚖ Act to support police officers but do not have the full powers of an officer.

⚖ Deal with minor offences.

⚖ Deter anti-social behaviour.

⚖ Guard crime scenes.

⚖ Provide crime prevention advice.

There are three main groupings of police officers, assisted by office support staff:

⚖ Uniformed branch, seen on the streets and the front-line investigators of crimes.

⚖ Traffic branch, enforces motoring regulations.

⚖ CID (Criminal Investigation Department), the plain-clothes branch that investigates more complex crimes.

The police investigate many types of crime. They use a lot of technology to help them identify criminals. The most recent advance has been the use of **DNA fingerprinting**, a forensic technique that has helped to solve many crimes by identifying suspects with great accuracy.

Scotland

Police services	8
Police officers	16,368
Support staff	7,901

Northern Ireland

Police services	1
Police officers	7,397
Support staff	2,701

Wales

Police services	4
Police officers	7,546
PCSOs	688
Support staff	3,754

England

Police services	39
Police officers	133,738
PCSOs	14,703
Support staff	72,235

The Court System

When someone has been charged with an offence, a court will decide whether the person is guilty or not guilty. There are different levels of court depending on the nature of the charge. In the court system there is overlap between the administration of criminal law and civil law. The diagram below shows the basic structure. The court system in Scotland is different.

Magistrates Court

Presided over by three magistrates or a district judge.

All criminal cases start in the Magistrates Court. More serious cases are transferred to the Crown Court.

The maximum sentence the court can impose is a fine of £5,000 (£2,000 in Northern Ireland) or six months in prison.

Some civil cases heard on debt, marriage problems and welfare of children.

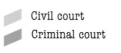

Civil court
Criminal court

Youth Court

Part of the Magistrates Court that deals with criminal offences committed by those aged 10 to 17.

Crown Court

Cases tried by a judge and jury.

Handles all serious criminal cases.

Hears appeals from the Magistrates Court.

Is able to impose more severe sentences than the Magistrates Court.

County Court

Main court for hearing civil cases.

Small claims court is part of the County Court.

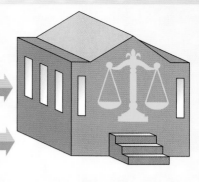

Judges and Law Lords outside the High Court in London.

The House of Lords

Hears **appeals** that relate to a point of law or of public importance.

Heard by a group of Law Lords.

From 2009 there will be a new Supreme Court. The Law Lords who now hear cases in the House of Lords will move to the Supreme Court. This will make the highest court in Britain clearly independent of Parliament.

Court of Appeal

Hears criminal and civil appeals against **convictions** or judgments made in the lower courts.

High Court

Hears civil cases and some criminal appeals.

Made up of three different 'divisions'.

The Family Division handles family matters from adoption to divorce.

The Queen's Bench Division deals with compensation claims, libel cases and contract law.

The Chancery Division deals with financial cases, from contested **wills** to tax issues.

Scotland's courts

⚖ District Court (being replaced by the Justice of the Peace Court) hears minor criminal cases.

⚖ Sheriff Court deals with criminal cases, such as theft or assault, and with civil cases. The **sheriff** is equivalent to a judge.

⚖ High Court of Justiciary is the highest criminal court and hears cases such as murder.

⚖ Court of Session is the highest civil court. It has two parts. The Outer House hears complex divorce cases and compensation cases. The Inner House hears appeals against judgments in the lower courts.

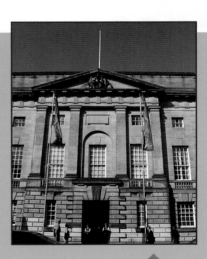

High Court of Justiciary, Edinburgh, Scotland.

Magistrates and Judges

The courts are run by magistrates and judges. They are the most important people in administering justice.

Magistrates

Magistrates or justices of the peace (JPs) are members of the public. Anyone can apply to be a magistrate, unless they have a criminal conviction or work in the police and related services. Magistrates serve in their local communities. They are not paid, and need to spend at least 26 half days in court every year. They receive legal advice from the Clerk to the Justices, a legal official at the court.

What does a magistrate do?

Magistrates sit at the local Magistrates Court. Three magistrates sit together, described as a **bench** of magistrates.

Judges

There are different levels of judges who carry out different tasks.

Lord Chief Justice

Head of all the judges in England and Wales.

Court of Appeal judges

The most senior judges. They hear appeals against the judgments of lower courts. They are based in London.

High Court judges

They hear the most complex criminal and civil cases. They are primarily based in London, but travel to major courts outside London for particular cases.

Circuit judges

The judges who hear cases at Crown Courts and County Courts. They work in particular regions of the country. Their name comes from the circuit they travelled to serve a number of different courtrooms.

Recorders

Part-time judges who hear the simplest of the Crown and County Court cases. This is the first step to being appointed a judge.

District judges (Magistrates Courts)

Full-time judges who sit by themselves in Magistrates Courts instead of a bench of magistrates. They sit where the courts are very busy, for example in large cities, or when there are complex cases to be heard. They mostly work in large cities. They used to be called stipendiary magistrates (the name came from the fact that they were paid a stipend, an old word for a salary).

The red robes of High Court judges who hear criminal cases.

Magistrates hear about 95 per cent of all criminal cases and:

⚖ Decide whether a defendant is innocent or guilty in cases of minor crime.

⚖ Sentence those they find guilty.

⚖ Hear requests for **bail** and for **remanding** a defendant in **custody**.

⚖ Sit on youth courts, dealing with cases against those under 18.

⚖ Hear family cases, dealing with marriage and other family matters.

⚖ Grant **search warrants** to the police to allow them to search a property as part of an investigation.

Why do judges wear wigs?

The most distinctive part of a judge's uniform is the wig. Before wigs became fashionable in the reign of Charles II (1660–85), judges did not wear wigs. Indeed they were slow to adopt the fashion. However, once established it has remained a symbol of a judge, even though wigs stopped being fashionable nearly 200 years ago.

How to address judges

The courtroom is a formal place. There are different levels of judge and this is reflected in how they are addressed.

High Court judges	My Lord/My Lady
Circuit judges	Your Honour
District judges	Sir/Madam
Magistrates	Your Worship or Sir/Madam

How a Court Works

In court the prosecution and the defence present their facts and arguments and the judge or jury decide on where the truth lies.

Criminal cases

For a case to come to court, the police present their evidence against the accused to the Crown Prosecution Service (CPS) (or, in Scotland, the Procurator Fiscal). If the CPS decides that the case has a reasonable chance of success, it is taken to court.

Inside a criminal court

1 **The judge** The judge controls the court. He decides on legal matters and guides the jury. If the jury finds the defendant guilty, the judge decides on the sentence. In Magistrates Courts the magistrates or the District Judge decide if the defendant is guilty (there is no jury) and also set the sentence.

4 **The jury** The jury is responsible for deciding whether the defendant is innocent or guilty. In law, the defendant is presumed to be innocent until proved guilty. The jury is made up of 12 individuals. Virtually everyone over 18 who is on the **electoral roll** can be called to serve on a jury. In Scotland the jury consists of 15 people and has to consider three verdicts, guilty, not guilty and not proven.

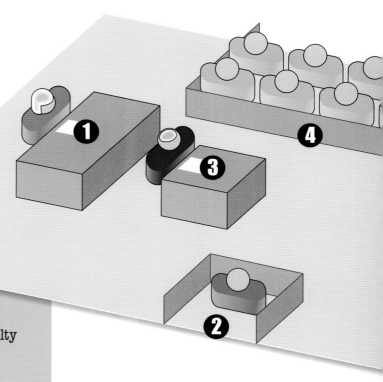

2 **Witnesses** A witness is someone who gives evidence in court. A witness may have seen the alleged crime or may have taken part in the investigation. A witness is not allowed to hear the case until after he or she has given evidence. An expert witness is someone with specialist knowledge that is relevant to the case.

3 **The clerk** The administrator of the court who makes sure a case runs smoothly.

Civil cases

Virtually all civil cases are held in front of a judge with no jury. Many disputes are settled before they reach court. The level of court that considers the case is usually decided on the size of the financial claim. The plaintiff and the defendant present their arguments and the judge decides where the truth lies. Not all civil cases are held in public.

5 The defence The lawyer who presents the case for the defendant to show that he or she is not guilty. The defence will call witnesses and will cross-examine prosecution witnesses.

6 The defendant He or she is the person accused of the crime being tried. The defendant sits in the **dock**, a secure part of the court.

At the trial the defendant will be asked if he or she pleads guilty or not guilty. If he or she pleads guilty, the judge then considers the sentence. If he or she pleads not guilty, then the prosecution and defence present their cases and the jury decides. The defendant does not have to give evidence in court.

8 The public gallery All criminal cases are carried out in public and any member of the public can watch a case.

7 The prosecutor The lawyer who presents the case for the prosecution. He or she will call witnesses to support the case and will cross-examine defence witnesses.

Punishments

When a defendant is found guilty in a criminal case, the sentence is the punishment that the judge or the magistrates hand out. In a civil case the judgment outlines any financial payments that the judge thinks appropriate. The criminal courts have a range of different punishments.

Fines

A **fine** is an amount of money that the guilty person has to pay to the State. The size of the fine relates to the seriousness of the crime. Some other official organisations can also impose fines – in 2007 the Office of Fair Trading imposed a fine of £121.5 million on British Airways for breaking competition law.

Prison

For the most serious crimes, people can be sent to prison. Removing a person's freedom is the most serious punishment that is allowed in Britain.

Community orders

For many offences, punishment within the community is more appropriate. Punishments that can form part of a community order include:

⚖️ **Supervision**, with regular meetings with an official called a **probation officer**. The probation officer advises and befriends the offender and can report problems to the courts.

⚖️ Banning, for example not being allowed to go to football matches.

⚖️ Unpaid work to help the local community.

⚖️ **Curfew**, requiring someone to be at a fixed place (usually home) at certain hours. **Electronic tags** can be fitted to offenders to enforce this.

An electronic tag can be used to check where an offender is.

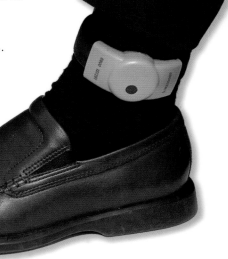

Suspended sentence

For prison sentences of one year or less the courts can suspend the sentence, which means the offender is supervised in the community rather than going to prison. If the offender breaks the terms of this community order, he can then be sent to prison.

ASBOs

ASBO is short for Anti-Social Behaviour Order. An ASBO requires someone to stop doing something that others think is anti-social. This can include:

- Disturbing neighbours (e.g. loud music, barking dogs).
- Gathering in groups outdoors and appearing to be threatening.
- Committing vandalism.
- Dumping rubbish and abandoning cars.

The orders are issued by civil courts. This means that the complaints against people do not have to be tested in the rigorous way that happens in criminal courts. If the order is broken, a prison sentence can be given.

Fixed penalties

Fixed penalty fines are given for various offences where the case is not taken to court. Parking fines and speeding fines are two examples.

How are sentences calculated?

The law lays down the maximum sentence for any particular offence. Guidelines indicate the variation in sentence that judges should consider. The judge (or magistrates) are responsible for each individual sentence. Both the prosecution and the defence can appeal against a sentence.

Examples

Crime: An assault that causes injury
Maximum sentence
5 years in prison

Planned (premeditated) assault causing serious injury or involving a weapon
2 to 4 years in prison

Planned assault causing relatively serious injury
36 months to 2 years in prison

Planned assault causing minor injury
12 to 36 weeks in prison

Unplanned assault causing minor, injury
Community Order to 26 weeks in prison

Further reductions can be considered if the defendant was provoked or caused an unintended injury. If the defendant pleads guilty, the judge reduces the sentence by between one-tenth and one-third, depending on when the defendant pleaded guilty.

Prisons

Prisons are used to detain those who have broken the law. Imprisonment has been used as a form of punishment for thousands of years.

How prisons used to be

In the nineteenth century, prisoners had to cope with a harsh regime. Some features of life at Inveraray prison in Scotland were:

⚖ One hour of exercise each day.

⚖ The first 30 days on a wooden bed with a wooden pillow.

⚖ Using the crank machine, a device where the prisoner had to turn round a handle for no useful purpose. The work could be made harder if the warder tightened a screw, the origin of the slang name for a prison warder.

Prisons today

Prison conditions have improved since then. There are also different levels of prison from maximum-security prisons for the most dangerous prisoners to open prisons, where prisoners have more freedoms. Prison life still revolves around an organised day. Sometimes prisoners spend most of the day locked up in their cells. Because of overcrowding many prisoners have to share cells.

The very strong door of the condemned cell at the old Newgate Prison in London.

⚖ It costs £41,000 to keep a person in prison for one year. A similar period on a community service order costs around £2,400.

⚖ One third of women prisoners had no previous convictions; only one-sixth of men had no previous convictions.

⚖ The average age for those starting a prison sentence is 27.

⚖ There are over 400 people over 70 in prison.

⚖ Around 150,000 children have a parent in prison.

⚖ Two-thirds of prisoners have a drug problem.

FACTS

How many people are in prison?

In England and Wales there are over 81,500 people in prison. In Scotland there are 7,600 prisoners and in Northern Ireland over 1,470.

Prisons in England and Wales are overcrowded, and the prison population may increase to around 96,000 by 2014. This means new prisons will have to be built. England and Wales have more prisoners for the size of the population than other countries in Europe. For every 100,000 people, there are 148 people in prison. In Norway there are 66.

Does prison work?

While in prison, criminals cannot commit offences. One purpose of prison is to persuade people not to commit crimes when they leave. Unfortunately the evidence is not encouraging:

- ⚖ 67 per cent of prisoners **re-offend** within two years of release.

- ⚖ Those jailed for six months or less do not receive **rehabilitation** and are more likely to re-offend.

- ⚖ For those serving community orders, 55 per cent re-offend within two years.

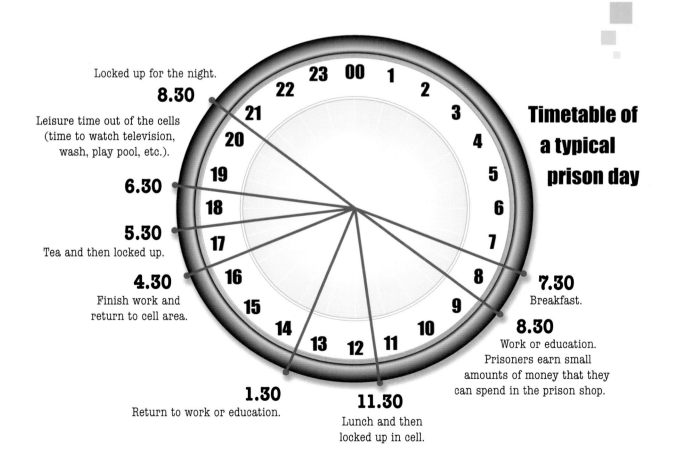

Timetable of a typical prison day

Locked up for the night.
8.30

Leisure time out of the cells (time to watch television, wash, play pool, etc.).
6.30

5.30
Tea and then locked up.

4.30
Finish work and return to cell area.

1.30
Return to work or education.

11.30
Lunch and then locked up in cell.

7.30
Breakfast.

8.30
Work or education. Prisoners earn small amounts of money that they can spend in the prison shop.

Human Rights

After the Second World War, the newly formed United Nations felt it was important that a list of the basic rights of individuals should be written down. The legal protection of an individual's rights have formed a key part of our legal system since 2000.

European Convention on Human Rights

This Convention was signed by European leaders on 4 November 1949. Britain formally agreed with it in 1951. However, it was not until 2000 that it became part of British law. From then on, all new legislation had to be in agreement with the convention and public bodies have to work within its terms (private companies are excluded). Individuals can challenge any enfringement of their rights, the final legal court being the European Court of Human Rights in Strasbourg.

But what are human rights?

As individuals, we have some fundamental expectations of the State and the public bodies that carry out the policies of the State:

- ⚖ The right to be treated fairly and with dignity.
- ⚖ The right to be safe and to be protected from harm.
- ⚖ The right to live the life we choose.
- ⚖ The right to take an active part in the community.

As well as rights, we have duties to respect the rights and freedom of others and to obey the laws of the community we live in.

Universal Declaration of Human Rights

This United Nations declaration was agreed on 10 December 1948 in Paris. Since then it has become the most translated document in the world, and is now available in over 336 languages. Article 1 starts:

'All human beings are born free and equal in dignity and rights.'

It establishes the basis of all other rights:

'Everyone has the right to life, liberty and security of person.'

In 30 brief clauses it states the fundamental rights and duties of all people. From this declaration have come more specific expressions of human rights.

Here are some situations from daily life, but remember in looking at them, that you must always respect the rights of others.

⚖️ You have the right to your own lifestyle and the way you look and dress.

⚖️ You have the right to practise your religion freely.

⚖️ The media do not have the right to look into your private life (the media will argue that they only do this when it is in the public interest).

⚖️ Any public body that holds your personal information should keep it securely and not share it without your permission.

⚖️ Public bodies should allow you to live in your home peacefully.

⚖️ The government cannot take away your freedom without good reason.

Human rights campaigns

We expect these rights to form the basis of a civilised society. While the rights of an individual are much greater in Britain than in some countries, not everything is as it should be. Consider these statements:

48 per cent of people feel that there is more racial prejudice than five years ago.

A quarter of Britain's population live below the poverty line.

A million homes in Britain are unfit to live in.

Campaigners believe that the human rights of these individuals affected are being infringed.

Where to seek help

The Equality and Human Rights Commission has been established by the British government to promote equality and human rights for all. They are there to help protect your rights.

Because more than half of young people leaving care have no GCSEs or GNVQs on leaving school

Because 24% of disabled people feel they are prisoners in their own home

Because 48% of people feel that there is more racial prejudice than there was five years ago

Because over a million houses in Britain are unfit to live in

The British Institute of HUMAN RIGHTS

Consumer Rights

When you buy something or make use of a service, you are a consumer. If something is wrong with your purchase or with the service provided, what can you do? The law provides some protection for you.

As a consumer you have these basic rights:

⚖ The right to choose how and where to purchase a product.

⚖ The right to accurate information about the product.

⚖ The right to know that the product is safe and will not cause any health problems.

⚖ The right to value for money.

⚖ The right to complain if a product does not work and to seek some form of compensation.

Who can help

There are many organisations which help protect the rights of the consumer.

⚖ The Office of Fair Trading, particularly concerned with ensuring that businesses trade fairly.

⚖ Consumer Direct, a telephone and online service provide by the Office of Fair Trading.

⚖ Trading Standards departments in local government, active in enforcing laws and regulations to protect consumers.

⚖ Trading Standards Institute, which provides a service for checking online sellers – Howard the Shopping Assistant.

Consumer rights are nothing new. There have always been problems with traders trying to get money from consumers unfairly. In the Magna Carta, signed by King John in 1215, he undertook that

> *'There shall be standard measures of wine, ale, and corn throughout the kingdom.'*

This was to stop people selling short measures. The consumer needs to know that a pint of beer sold in London is the same size as one sold in Glasgow.

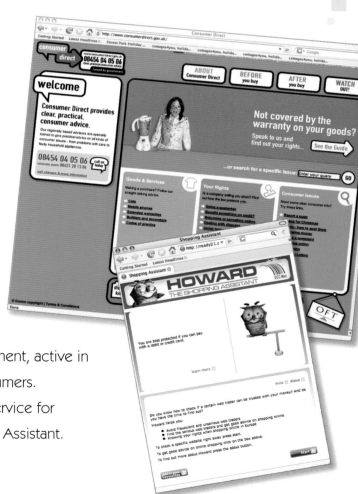

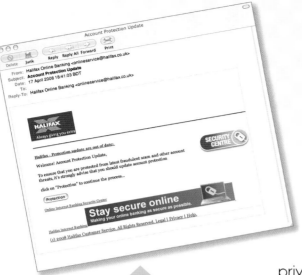

Scams

A scam is when someone is tricked into paying more for something than it is worth or providing private information to people who are not entitled to it. For example, a workman may offer to repair someone's house, do the work badly and then charge an excessive price. Scams have spread to the internet, where offers are made that seem too good to be true or which try to steal valuable information (bank account details, for example). Internet scams are very difficult to control because it is hard to find out who is doing them and in which country they are based.

If you have any problems contact www.consumerdirect.gov.uk for advice.

One scam is to make people believe a request for information is genuine. This e-mail looks official but, in fact, had nothing to do with the Halifax bank.

Ombudsman

The person to complain to about poor service from a government department and from many professions is called an **ombudsman**. It is a strange word. It comes from the Swedish word that originally meant representative, and was used to describe the first appointed Ombudsman to the Swedish Parliament in 1809. The first ombudsman in Britain was the Parliamentary Ombudsman, who was appointed in 1967.

Top ten complaints received by Consumer Direct in 2007

1. Second-hand cars purchased from independent dealers
2. Mobile phones (service agreements)
3. TVs
4. Mobile phones (hardware)
5. Personal goods and services
6. General building work
7. Car repairs and servicing from independent garages
8. Upholstered furniture
9. Internet service providers
10. Second-hand cars purchased from franchised dealers

Crime in the UK

Is crime increasing? Is crime decreasing? These questions are argued over endlessly. What is undoubtedly true is that the types of crime committed keep changing and that some crimes increase while others decrease.

Overall recorded crime has been decreasing in the last 10 years. The British Crime Survey for England and Wales includes both crimes reported to the police and crimes that people have suffered but have not reported (many cases of vandalism, for example). In 1995 over 19 million crimes were recorded. By 2005 this had fallen to just over 11 million, a fall of around 40 per cent. In the same period there were around 5.4 million crimes reported to the police in England and Wales.

Of these crimes about 1.5 million were solved.

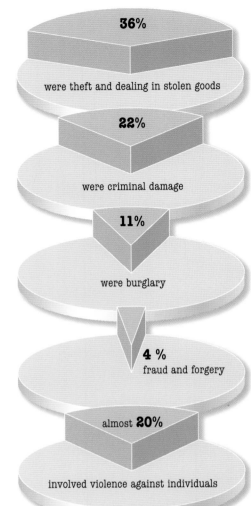

36% were theft and dealing in stolen goods

22% were criminal damage

11% were burglary

4 % fraud and forgery

almost 20% involved violence against individuals

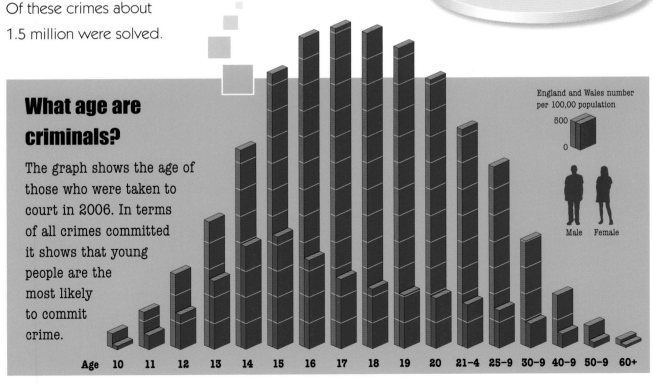

What age are criminals?

The graph shows the age of those who were taken to court in 2006. In terms of all crimes committed it shows that young people are the most likely to commit crime.

England and Wales number per 100,00 population

500

0

Male   Female

Age 10 11 12 13 14 15 16 17 18 19 20 21-4 25-9 30-9 40-9 50-9 60+

Were things better in the past?

Look at the comments below. The only surprise is the date they were made. People have always felt threatened by young people, but forget that young people are major victims of crime as well.

"the manners of children are deteriorating. . . the child of today is coarser, more vulgar, less refined than his parents were".
Mr Heathcote, a Brighton magistrate, 1898

"The passing of parental authority, the absence of restraint, the wildness of extremes, the confusion of unrelated liberties, are but a few characteristics of after-war conditions".
James Butterworth, in 1932.

The crimes that no one notices

Some researchers asked 1,800 people in England and Wales about 'middle-class' crime. They discovered that:

⚖ 34 per cent paid people in cash so that they could avoid paying tax.

⚖ 32 per cent kept the money when they were given too much change.

⚖ 18 per cent had taken something home from work.

⚖ 7 per cent claimed more than they should on an insurance claim.

⚖ 5 per cent claimed for refunds they knew they were not entitled to.

Court statistics

In 2006:

⚖ 962,000 offenders were fined.

⚖ 191,000 offenders given community sentences.

⚖ 96,000 offenders given prison sentences.

Discussion Points

Here are a few suggestions for discussion points on law and order in Britain (the page numbers indicate where the topic is covered in the book).

● What laws would you like Parliament to make? (**page 4**)

● What are the main differences between criminal law and civil law? (**pages 6–9**)

● Who does what in a courtroom, and how might each person feel? (**pages 16–17**) Have a look at the www.cjsonline.gov.uk website described opposite. This will give you the chance to see some real courtrooms.

● What sort of person do you think would make a good magistrate? (**pages 14–15**)

● Should judges stop wearing wigs? Some judges think so and others think not. What do you think? (**page 15**)

● In England and Wales juries can find someone either guilty or not guilty. In Scotland they have three choice, guilty, not guilty and not proven. Why do you think a verdict of 'not proven' might be needed? (**pages 16–17**)

● Do you think judges should be able to vary the sentences for the same crime? (**page 19**)

● A variety of different punishments are described on **pages 18–21**? Which do you think would be most likely to stop people re-offending?

● 'Everyone has the right to life, liberty and security of person.' So says the Universal Declaration of Human Rights. How well do we live up to this in our country? What about other countries in the world? (**pages 22–23**)

● Look at the chart on **page 26** that shows the age of offenders. Why do you think that so many crimes are committed by teenagers?

Websites

For information on the law and how it affects you, visit: **www.rizer.co.uk**

Many of the official legal sites are designed for adult use. Of these the Criminal Justice online site is approachable, complete with interactive walkthroughs of a court for jurors, victims, witnesses and defendants It shows the inside of a number of actual courtrooms. It also has a section on offenders, with an interactive prison walkthrough. All the areas can be accessed from the tabs on the home page.

www.cjsonline.gov.uk

To find out more about what judges do visit:
www.judiciary.gov.uk

To find out more about life in an old jail (and about the court house next to it) visit:
www.inverarayjail.co.uk/

To discover more about the universal declaration of Human Rights, visit:
www0.un.org/cyberschoolbus/humanrights/

To read the declaration, go to:
www.un.org/Overview/rights.html

To find out more about human rights in Britain, visit:
www.yourrights.org.uk/

If you want to find out more about consumer rights, visit:
www.consumerdirect.gov.uk/

And if you need help with a particular problem, try Howard the Shopper's Assistant, provided by the Trading Standards Institute:
www.ukecc.net/sub.asp?id=209

Note to parents and teachers: Every effort has been made by the Publishers to ensure that these websites are suitable for children, that they are of the highest educational value, and that they contain no inappropriate or offensive material. However, because of the nature of the Internet, it is impossible to guarantee that the contents of these sites will not be altered. We strongly advise that Internet access is supervised by a responsible adult.

Glossary

adoption The process by which a couple legally take a child into their family when they are not parents of the child.

Anti-Social Behaviour Order An order made by the civil court to stop someone repeating a particular anti-social action.

appeal To request a court to look again at a verdict or sentence.

arrest The police arrest someone when they think he or she may have committed a crime and they wish to question them.

bail After someone is charged with an offence but before the case comes to court, the defendant can be granted bail. This means that they can live at home so long as they obey certain conditions set by the court. Compare with remand.

barrister A lawyer who prosecutes or defends cases in the higher courts (the Crown Court and the High Court). Compare with solicitor.

bench (of magistrates) The term used to describe the three magistrates who sit together in a magistrates court.

case The name given to a particular legal trial or other legal matter.

charge The formal accusation made by the police against someone who they think has committed a crime.

community order A sentence that provides punishment within the community rather than in prison.

conviction The outcome of a case when the defendant is found guilty.

curfew An order to be inside your home or some other specified place at particular times.

custody This describes when a defendant is held in prison between being charged and appearing in court. Compare with bail.

damages An outcome in a civil case when the judge orders a payment of money to be made by one side in the case to the other.

detain To keep someone in prison on the order of a court.

DNA fingerprinting Each of us has a unique DNA pattern. DNA evidence left at the scene of a crime can be used to identify people who were there more successfully than traditional identification by fingerprints.

dock The place in a the courtroom where the defendant sits.

electoral roll A listing of everyone over the age of 17 who can vote at elections.

electronic tag A device attached to a convicted criminal that establishes where that person is at any time.

guilty The decision of the jury or of magistrates that someone has committed the crime he or she was charged with.

innocent Describing someone who has not committed an offence. In British law, anyone charged with an offence is assumed to be innocent until a jury or magistrates have decided that the person is guilty..

judgment The legal ruling of a judge at the end of a case.

magistrate A member of the local community who, with two others, decides on most criminal charges in a Magistrates Court.

mediator A person who is skilled in resolving disputes without involving the civil courts.

offence The name give to a particular criminal act.

ombudsman A person people can complain to about poor service from the government or poor advice from professionals.

plaintiff The person who brings a civil case against someone else.

probation officer An official who works with offenders in the community.

rehabilitation The process of helping criminals not to commit further crimes.

remand Being held in prison between being charged and being tried.

re-offend To commit another crime having already been convicted for a crime.

search warrant The official permission needed from magistrates by the police to search a suspect's house.

sentence The punishment for someone convicted of a crime.

sheriff In Scotland, the name for the judge in the Sheriff Court.

solicitor A lawyer who deals directly with clients (members of the public). He may ask a barrister to represent a client in court.

supervision The keeping of a check on how an offender is behaving.

will A legal statement of what someone wants to happen to their possessions when they die.

Index